D1520263

Mary
Stories
from the Bible

Under the direction of Romain Lizé, Executive Vice President, MAGNIFICAT
Editor, MAGNIFICAT: Isabelle Galmiche
Editor, Ignatius: Vivian Dudro
Translator: Janet Chevrier
Proofreader: Claire Gilligan
Assistant to the Editor: Pascale van de Walle
Layout Designers: Armelle Riva, Jean-Marc Richard
Production: Thierry Dubus, Sabine Marioni

Original French edition: *Belles Histoires pour s'endormir avec Marie*
© 2013 by Mame, Paris.
© 2018 by MAGNIFICAT, New York • Ignatius Press, San Francisco
All rights reserved.   7378075
ISBN Ignatius Press 978-1-62164-254-1 • ISBN MAGNIFICAT 978-1-941709-64-1

Mary
Stories
from the Bible

Text by Charlotte Grossetête

Illustrations by Sibylle Delacroix,
Dominique Mertens, and Éric Puybaret

MAGNIFICAT · IGNATIUS

Contents

p. 7
The Childhood of Mary

Text: Charlotte GROSSETÊTE
Illustrations: Madeleine BRUNELET

p. 15
The Annunciation

Text: Charlotte GROSSETÊTE
Illustrations: Dominique MERTENS

p. 23
The Birth of Jesus

Text: Charlotte GROSSETÊTE
Illustrations: Éric PUYBARET

p. 31
The Wedding Feast at Cana

Text: Charlotte GROSSETÊTE
Illustrations: Dominique MERTENS

p. 41
The Death and Resurrection of Jesus

Text: Charlotte GROSSETÊTE
Illustrations: Éric PUYBARET

That morning, when Joachim came home from the Temple, his wife, Anne, could tell right away that he was upset. They had been married for so long, she could read his face like a book.

"What's the matter?" she asked him.

Joachim hesitated to answer. He didn't want to hurt her feelings. But then he said, "The high priest just sent me away. He doesn't want me to serve among the priests at the Temple anymore."

"But why?!" exclaimed Anne.

"Because we've never been able to have children," Joachim replied. "He thinks God has cursed us."

This story is not found in Scripture; it is inspired by an ancient tradition in the Church, both East and West, about Mary's parentage and girlhood.

Anne was a strong woman, but at these words, she broke down in tears.

"It's so unfair to say such a thing! I'm sure that God loves us. We've always served him faithfully with all our hearts. And his love is infinite."

Joachim hugged her tightly in his arms to comfort her. Then he said with a sigh, "I'm going to go spend some time in the desert. I need to pray. In the silence of the desert, I feel closer to God."

And Joachim did as he said. He spent forty days in solitary prayer from morning to night. He had a heavy heart, but he trusted in God and called on his help.

At the end of forty days, an angel appeared to him.

"Joachim," said the angel, "the Lord has heard your prayers; Anne has been praying night and day at home. How right you both were to trust in God's love! Blessed are you! You will soon have a child, a little girl unlike any other, for she is destined for a remarkable role in God's plan of salvation."

When the angel left him, Joachim hurried back to Jerusalem. As he was reaching the Golden Gate into the city, Anne ran to meet him and threw herself into his arms. They were so happy to be together again!

Some time later, Anne gave birth to a little girl, whom they called Mary. When the high priest heard of the birth, he called Joachim back to the Temple and awkwardly apologized. "Forgive me for sending you away. Please come join us again."

The other priests nodded their heads in agreement. One of them said, "We miss you. You have always been a model servant of God."

Time went by. Mary grew up, never giving her parents the slightest trouble: no tantrums, no sulks. She was lively and amusing. She was mischievous sometimes, but never unkind. Her heart was as pure as newly fallen snow.

Anne was sometimes puzzled that her little girl spent so many hours in her room. Curiosity finally got the better of Anne. One day she crept around to the back of the house to peek through the window. There was Mary on her knees! Mary was so rapt in prayer, she did not even notice her mother.

Anne said to Joachim, "What a joy to see Mary so close to God! It's clear that she is a gift from heaven."

Joachim replied, "Prayer is preparing her heart for the special mission foretold by the angel."

"Yes..." said Anne, lost in thought.

At that very moment, Mary burst into the room.

"It's time for our visit to the poor, Daddy. Are you coming?"

Joachim cheerfully got up. Every afternoon, they would go together to distribute food to the poor. Before Mary was born, Joachim had done the rounds all alone. But now he had his daughter to take with him. Or rather, it was Mary who took him, always wanting to go farther and visit longer. It was their favorite outing.

Anne handed Mary the basket of food she had prepared and watched them go with a smile.

"Don't wear your poor old father out!" she shouted. "Yesterday evening he came home exhausted!"

Mary turned and waved goodbye, saying, "I promise, Mommy!"

And Anne waved back thinking, "That girl really is full of grace!"

Since Anne and Joachim had moved to Nazareth, more than one young man in the village had asked for Mary's hand in marriage, for she had grown into a stunning young woman. She turned heads as she went by to draw water from the well. Even more than her beauty, it was her gentleness and her smile that captured everyone's heart.

Joachim and Anne finally accepted Joseph the carpenter's marriage proposal. He seemed to them the best match for Mary: first, because he loved God with all his soul, and, then—though to Anne and Joachim this wasn't as important—because he was a descendant of King David.

Mary was delighted with her parents' choice. A tall, strapping fellow, Joseph was as solid as the wood he worked with. She felt she could love and trust him. She was sure of it: they would be very happy together in the sight of the Lord!

One morning, she was busy sewing linens for their future home. She had just put out the lamp, for the dawn light now flooded the room. As she worked, Mary listened to the chirping of the birds awakening the countryside and thought about her Joseph.

"I'll go visit him at his workshop later," she thought happily to herself.

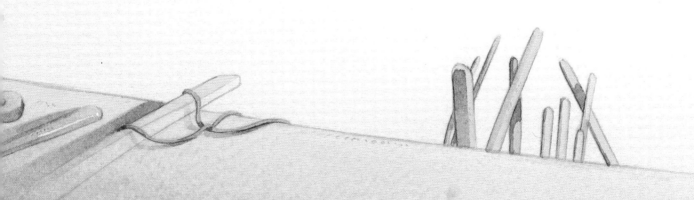

Suddenly, Mary sensed that someone else was in the room, someone who hadn't come in through the door. She looked up at a light-filled face and knew that it was an angel.

"Rejoice, Mary, full of grace, the Lord is with you," said the angel Gabriel as he bowed before the young woman.

In amazement, Mary dropped her needle and thread. The messenger of God went on, "Do not be afraid, Mary, for you have found favor with the Lord. You are to have a son, whom you will name Jesus."

As her eyes widened with astonishment, Mary stammered, "How shall this be? I'm not married yet!"

The angel Gabriel replied, "The Holy Spirit will come upon you, and the power of the Most High will overshadow you. That is why your child will be called the Son of God."

Mary was speechless. The angel went on, "Your cousin Elizabeth, the one everyone calls barren, is also expecting a son even though she is old, for nothing is impossible for God!"

"I am the handmaid of the Lord; may everything happen to me as you say!"

With that, the angel disappeared. Mary sat for a long while thinking about what had just happened, repeating to God, "Yes...yes!" Then she remembered her fiancé, Joseph, and got up to go tell him the wonderful news; but once outside, she was seized with worry.

"How can I explain this to Joseph? What will he think when he finds out I'm expecting a baby? God alone can break such news to him!"

So Mary went in haste to the hill country where Elizabeth and her husband, Zechariah, lived. She needed to talk to her cousin about this miracle that was happening to both of them.

When she arrived at Elizabeth's house, Mary gave her a hug and admired her growing tummy. Filled with emotion, Elizabeth held her in her arms, saying, "How wonderful that the mother of my Lord should come to visit me! When you arrived, I could feel my baby leap for joy inside me!"

With that, a song of great praise rose to Mary's lips: "My soul magnifies the Lord! He has looked down upon his handmaid, and he has done great things for me. All generations will for ever call me blessed!"

Mary stayed some time with Elizabeth and Zechariah. She often thought about Joseph and hoped that he would not be sad or worried that she had left.

At first Joseph was confused about Mary, but then one night an angel appeared to him in a dream and explained everything. From then on, Joseph awaited Mary's return with trust, marveling at the great adventure that God had in store for them.

The Birth of Jesus

"By order of the emperor of Rome..."

When this cry echoed through the town square, the villagers of Nazareth rushed to hear the news. Mary arrived last, for she was expecting her baby very soon and walked more slowly than everyone else.

When everyone had quieted down, the messenger continued the proclamation: "By order of Caesar Augustus, the population of the empire is to be counted. To do this, each inhabitant must go to be enrolled in his town of origin."

Mary turned to her husband, Joseph, who was also listening to the announcement, his carpentry tools in hand. He looked at her in dismay. His town of origin was Bethlehem, the city of King David.

"Do we really have to travel so far? What if the baby is born along the way?" Mary whispered.

"I'm afraid we must," said Joseph with a sigh. "You don't argue with an order of the emperor."

So Mary and Joseph set off, in the chill of winter. The road was packed with crowds of other people also traveling to their native towns. The donkey on which Joseph had seated Mary snorted impatiently. Mary was uncomfortable and tired, but she bravely endured the long, slow journey without complaint.

At last they arrived in sight of Bethlehem! Taking the donkey by the bridle, Joseph hurried it along, for night was falling and the air was turning bitterly cold. They knew they had to find shelter quickly!

Just as they were entering the town, Mary murmured in a worried voice, "I can feel the baby coming..."

Joseph hurried to the only inn in Bethlehem and pounded at the door.

"Who's that at this time of night?" shouted the innkeeper.

"Joseph of Nazareth. I've come to enroll for the census and—"

"You're not the only one!" grumbled the innkeeper. "There are no more rooms in the inn. I've even got people sleeping on the floor! Go find somewhere else."

"But my wife is about to give birth!" Joseph insisted.

The innkeeper shook his head: "I'm very sorry, Mister, but there's really no more room here."

With that, he slammed the door. There stood Joseph and Mary, alone under the starry sky. Joseph laid his hand on Mary's shoulder. "Don't worry. I'll find us a place."

After searching a while, Joseph found a stable with an ox inside. It wasn't much, but it was quiet. He spread a bunch of hay on the ground and gently laid Mary upon it. She thanked him with a little smile.

In the middle of the night, Mary gave birth to her son, Jesus. She wrapped him in swaddling clothes and laid him in the manger. Kneeling in the hay, Mary and Joseph gazed in silent wonder at the holy child.

Suddenly, a great noise of footsteps and bleating broke the silence. A bunch of shepherds clattered into the stable. The oldest greeted Mary and explained, "An angel appeared to us on the hillside where we were watching over our flocks. He proclaimed to us that a Savior had just been born here. We've hurried here to see the infant!"

"Shh!" ordered one little shepherd. "You'll wake the baby!"

In silence, the shepherds went down on their knees before Jesus, and the sheep gathered around the manger.

The lambs stood as still as the men. Not a sound could be heard but the breathing of the ox warming the baby.

As Mary raised her eyes to heaven to give thanks to God, she noticed a great star moving through the night sky, as though it were moving closer to Bethlehem. Joseph saw it, too, and on the evenings that followed, he watched its progress with curiosity.

"It's closer than it was yesterday," he said each night.

The mysterious star at last came to rest over Bethlehem. As it did, a most curious thing happened. Three travelers dressed in luxurious robes entered the stable. As Mary rocked the baby Jesus in her arms, he waved his little hand with a smile as though he had been expecting these strangers.

The Magi, wise men from the East, made a deep bow and laid three costly gifts at the feet of Jesus: gold, frankincense, and myrrh.

" Thank you," Mary said to them.

"It is we who thank you," replied the Magi, "for you have given birth to the one who shall be King of all the world."

The baby born in Bethlehem grew up in Nazareth, his parents' village. Joseph and Mary raised him there with love, and Jesus grew in strength and in wisdom until he reached manhood.

The Wedding Feast at Cana

It was a day of celebration in the village of Cana. Two young people had gotten married, and everyone was full of joy. The bride, lovely in her wedding dress, was moving from table to table greeting the guests when she stopped in front of a woman dressed in blue.

"Mary!" she exclaimed. "Thank you for coming all the way from Nazareth!"

"I would have traveled farther than that for such a great day," replied Mary. "Jesus and I are pleased to be here."

"Your son is here too?" asked the bride.

Mary pointed to a man in a white tunic chatting with friends at a neighboring table. "That's him," she said.

"I would never have recognized him!" said the bride. "It's been such a long time since I last saw him."

Mary nodded, "Yes, he's a grown man now. He's come with some disciples who have been following him for several days now."

At that moment, an old man cried out, "Waiter, more wine! My glass is empty!"

As the bride moved on, Mary watched the waiter approaching. He was staring into the bottom of his jug with a worried look. Why did he seem so troubled when everyone was having such a good time? He poured the jug, but after just a few drops, there was no more wine.

"I'm sorry," stammered the waiter, "the jug is empty."

"Well, go and fill it up again!" the old man snapped impatiently.

"Yes, of course," said the waiter.

He went off. Mary could see him showing the jug to another servant, and overheard the second servant's reply. "What a disaster! We don't have any more wine, and the guests will surely soon start to notice."

Mary went to Jesus, who was still talking with his friends. She put her hand on his shoulder and whispered, "They have no more wine."

Jesus looked into his mother's eyes. "Why are you telling me this, Mother? My hour has not yet come."

Mary said nothing, but her look spoke volumes. It was as though she were saying, "I know that you can do something." Jesus saw that his friends were curious. They looked at Mary, then at their empty cups; then they looked to him, so he got up from the table.

Mary immediately went to find the waiters. She pointed Jesus out to them, just as he was slipping away to the back of the house.

"Do whatever he tells you," she told them.

The surprised servants caught up with Jesus. He was standing before six huge, empty stone jars. He said to the two servants, "Fill these jars with water."

The servants hesitated. That would take them some time, and they wondered what good it would do anyway. Mary's instructions had been very clear, so they obeyed. When they were done, Jesus said, "Now draw some out and go serve it to the master of the banquet."

The servant went to the table of honor with a full jug. The master of the banquet, busy chatting to the groom, hadn't noticed that his cup was empty. He absently held it out to the waiter. As the liquid began to flow, the waiter almost dropped the jug. It was wine! The master of the banquet tasted it, opened his eyes wide, and turned to the groom, saying, "How unusual! Normally, people serve the best wine first, and once the guests have had plenty to drink, they bring out the cheaper wine. But you have saved the best for last. I've never tasted wine so delicious! Where have you been hiding it?"

The servants were bursting to tell what had happened, but Jesus, raising his finger to his lips, said, "Shh!"

And the master of the banquet raised his glass to make a toast, "Long live the newlyweds. May their love be as perfect as this extraordinary wine!"

Everyone applauded. The servants then began filling all the guests' glasses, but they were no longer worried and joined in the general rejoicing. Yes, everyone was very, very happy indeed!

The Death and Resurrection of Jesus

Mary was standing at the foot of the cross. It was the saddest day of her life: her son was dying. Raising her head, she could see Jesus' face looking down on her and on all the world. With his arms outstretched, he seemed to be embracing the entire earth before returning to his Father. Mary understood that he was freely giving up his life for the salvation of mankind.

But it was so cruel! She recalled the morning she presented her baby in the Temple in Jerusalem. An old man named Simeon took Jesus in his arms and proclaimed that he was the promised Savior. Then he said to Mary, "One day, you will suffer greatly because of your child; a sword of sorrow will pierce your heart."

Thirty-three years later, on this terrible Friday, Simeon's words had come true. Mary suffered to the depths of her soul. But she knew that the love and the grace of God are stronger than death.

Struggling to tear her eyes away from Jesus, she looked at the crowd gathered nearby. There were stern soldiers and enemies of Jesus who had come to watch him die. These men were mocking him. Others were crying because they knew that Jesus had done no wrong. Among them were people Jesus had healed.

Above Mary's head a voice cried out, "For myself, I deserve my punishment; but this man is innocent. Jesus, remember me when you enter your Kingdom!"

Mary raised her eyes to the man speaking. He was one of the thieves being crucified next to Jesus. Jesus looked at him tenderly and said, "This day you will be with me in heaven."

Mary looked at John, Jesus' best friend, standing next to her. All the other disciples had kept their distance, for fear of being arrested. But John had said to Mary, "Even if I must die, I will never abandon your son."

John had kept his word. After Jesus' trial, he had given Mary his arm and accompanied her to the top of Mount Calvary. Thanks to him, Mary felt a little less alone at the moment when Jesus was about to give up his life.

Suddenly, a cry came from the cross.

"Mother..."

Overcome with emotion, Mary raised her eyes.

"Mother, behold your son," said Jesus as he nodded his head toward John.

Then he gasped, "John, here is your mother."

John's eyes opened wide; and, for the first time since Jesus' arrest, Mary could see a little glimmer of hope shining. John now knew that life would go on, since Jesus had entrusted his mother to him. As for Mary, she understood very well that by asking her to adopt John, Jesus was asking her to become the mother of all God's children.

In the middle of the afternoon, darkness covered the land. A last cry rose up from the cross: "Father, into your hands I commend my spirit!" With that, Jesus breathed his last.

Mary took John's hand and squeezed it hard. They waited for the soldiers to take Jesus' body down, and together accompanied it to the tomb. Then John took Mary to his home, and they prayed together through the silent hours of the night.

At sunrise on Sunday morning, some women who were friends of Jesus came knocking at the door and, without even waiting to be let in, rushed inside, trembling with emotion.

"We've just come back from the cemetery. Jesus' tomb is empty! An angel told us that he is risen!"

At these words, John left Mary at home and ran to the tomb to see if this good news could really be true. He returned breathless, his eyes shining with heavenly light. "Mother!" he gasped. "I saw the empty tomb. Your son is truly risen! He is alive!"

That same day Jesus appeared to his disciples, including John and, one may suppose, his mother.

As John and Mary looked after each other, the spirit of Jesus remained among them, for Jesus had promised his disciples, "Where two or three of you are gathered in my name, there am I in the midst of them."

Printed in June 2018 by Tien Wah Press, Malaysia
Job number MGN 18014
Printed in compliance with the Consumer Protection Safety Act, 2008